How to increase
Sales
using Pinterest.

Claretta T. Pam

Claretta T. Pam

How to increase sales using *Pinterest*

Claretta T. Pam

How to increase sales using Pinterest. Entrepreneurial Universe Series (Volume 3)

Help Us Keep This Guide Up to Date

Every effort has been made by the author and editors to make this guide as accurate and useful as possible. However, many changes can occur after a guide is published.
We would like to hear from you concerning your experiences with this guide and how you feel it could be improved and be kept up to date. While we may not be able to respond to all comments and suggestions, we'll take all correspondence to heart and make certain to share them with the author. Please send your comments and suggestions to the following address:

Innovative Publishers Inc.
Double Click Press
Book ID #4705120
PO Box 300446
Boston, MA 02130

or you may email us at corrections@innovative-publishers.com

Claretta T. Pam

Cover art and design provided by
Taylor Pam — Fine Art LLC

Art available for purchase at
http://taylorpam.artistwebsites.com/featured/fractal-015-taylor-pam.html

How to increase sales using Pinterest

Copyright © 2014 by Claretta Pam

Innovative Publishers, Inc. & Double Click Press and colophon are trademarks of Open Nebula LLC, Intellectual Property Series.

Published and printed in the United States by
Innovative Publishers, Inc., Boston, Massachusetts

Innovative Publishers

Double Click Press

Claretta T. Pam

ISBN-10: 1-4913-2360-4   ISBN-13: 978-1-4913-2360-1 Paperback
ISBN-10: 1-4913-2365-5   ISBN-13: 978-1-4913-2365-6 Hardback
ISBN-10: 1-4913-2370-1   ISBN-13: 978-1-4913-2370-0 Kindle
ISBN-10: 1-4913-2375-2   ISBN-13: 978-1-4913-2375-5 iBook
ISBN-10: 1-4913-2380-9   ISBN-13: 978-1-4913-2380-9 Nook
ISBN-10: 1-4913-2385-X   ISBN-13: 978-1-4913-2385-4 AudioBook

Library of Congress Cataloging-in-Publication Data

Library of Congress Cataloging-in-Publication Data

Pam, Claretta, 1969-
   How to increase sales using Pinterest / Claretta Pam. -- First edition.
      pages cm. -- (Entrepreneurial universe series ; 3)
   ISBN 978-1-4913-2360-1 (pb : alk. paper) -- ISBN 978-1-4913-2365-6 (hb : alk.
paper) -- ISBN 978-1-4913-2370-0 (ebook) -- ISBN 978-1-4913-2375-5 (ebook) -- ISBN
978-1-4913-2385-4 (audiobk) -- ISBN 978-1-4913-2380-9 (ebook)
   1. Pinterest. 2. Internet marketing. I. Title.
   HF5415.1265.P365 2014
   658.8'72--dc23
                                                           2014011079

10 9 8 7 6 5 4 3 2 1   14 15 16 17 18

An interpretation of the printing code: is the number of the books printing. The rightmost number of the second series of numbers is the year of the books printing. For example, a printing code of 1–14 shows that the first printing occurred in 2014.

First edition. July 2014

For general information on our other products and services or for technical support, please contact our technical support within the United States at admin@innovative-publishers.com online at http://innovative-publishers.com.

Titles Forthcoming:

How to make money using Facebook

How to make money using LinkedIn

How to make money using YouTube

How to make money using Twitter

DEDICATION

To the entrepreneur that meets the challenge to follow their dreams.

Table of Contents

ACKNOWLEDGMENTS

CHAPTER 1

Getting Started

What is Pinterest all about?

Pinterest is a popular social network which allows users globally to share and connect. People can initiate projects and collect ideas related to their hobbies and interests. In addition, it has become a monumental vehicle for the expression of creativity in different realms. People using Pinterest can derive inspiration and generate ideas by looking at the works and plans of others. It serves as a visual idea sharing machine and capitalizes on the concept of saving ideas for later use. The word, Pinterest, itself is an eclectic wordplay which means that you can literally pin your interests in an online forum like you would in real life on a notice board.

How it Works

The way Pinterest works is slightly different because for the creation of an account you need to send in a request on their website or ask a friend to send you an invitation. After this you can install the 'Pin It' button in your browser toolbar, which helps you pin things online directly. You can also upload items from your computer and simply copy paste the link of the site and Pinterest will give you the option of pinning items on that site.

Whatever ideas or images you have pinned online can be organized comprehensively into categories called Boards. You can add plans on your boards, share it publically or even keep it a secret. Similarly, it is very easy to follow other boards. When you follow a person or a specific board, the pins will appear on your newsfeed. The items pinned will appear with a visual bookmark on your board.

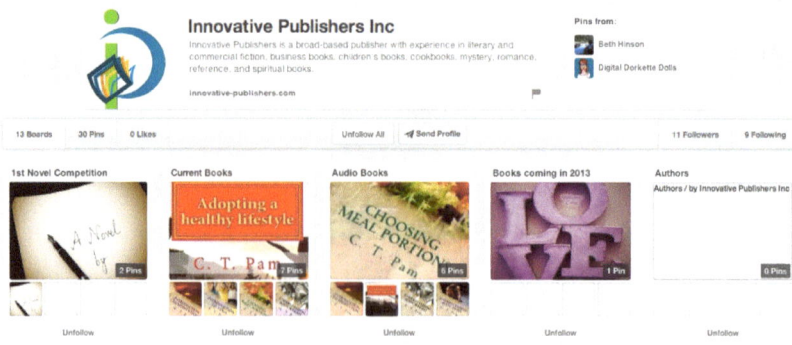

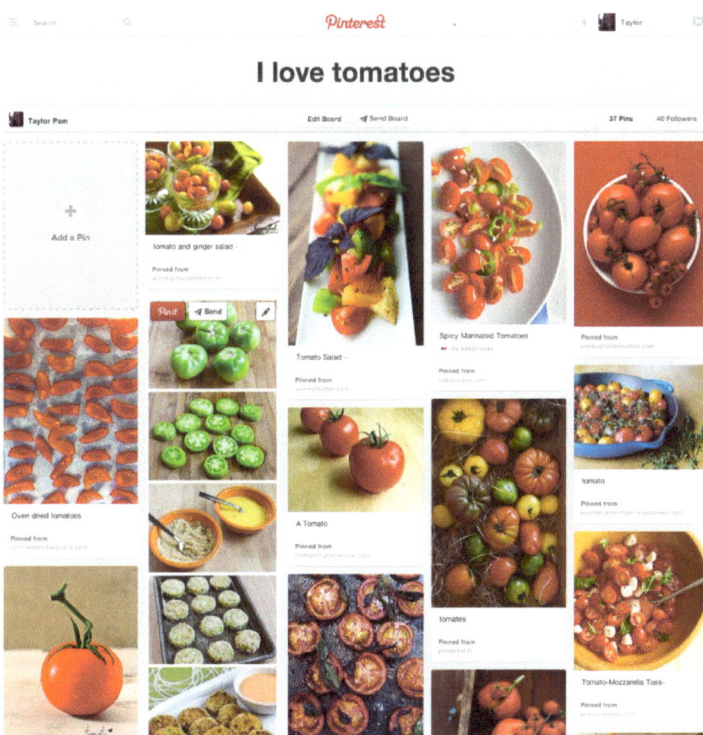

You can also explore the vast varieties of recipes, tips, trips, ideas and guides pinned by others and even save them to your own board by using the option of 'Repin'. Repinning is a refreshing new way of sharing and showing appreciation for people's creativity.

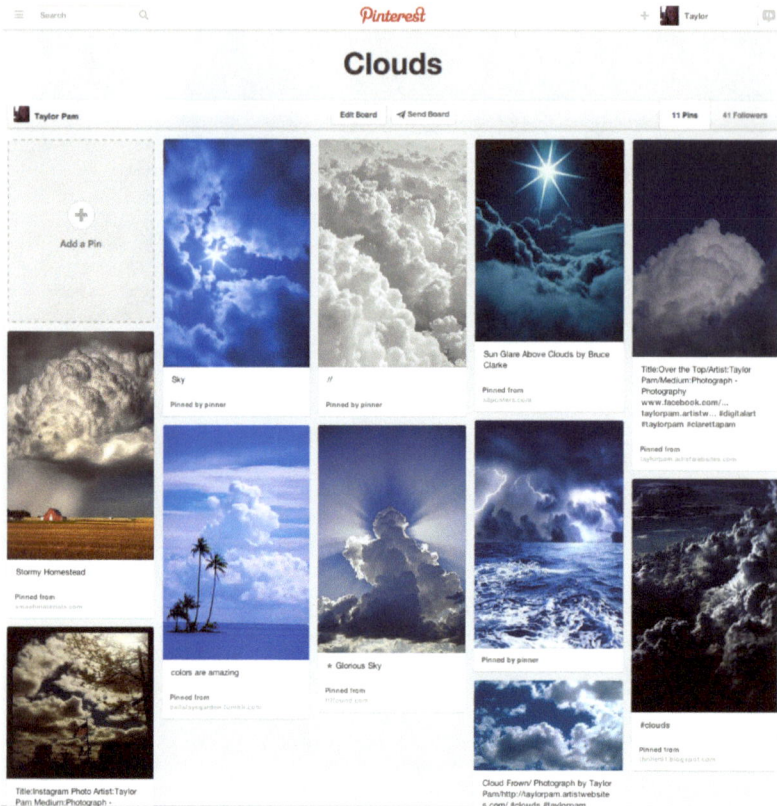

Functions of Pinterest

Previously, whenever you would surf the web, you would have to save things on your computer for later use; for instance, a home decoration tutorial or a DIY jewelry lesson, anything which interested you had to be saved. Pinterest makes this process intuitive and productive by allowing you to pin the visual ideas online onto your personal board provided in your account.

Not only can you save ideas, you can also share them with your friends. Like other social networking sites, people on Pinterest have accounts, timelines, newsfeeds and followers.

Another very important purpose Pinterest serves is that it may increase the popularity of your blog, Facebook page, Instagram, or LinkedIn postings. As a blogger or poster, you can access the wide audience on Pinterest by simply pinning the content of your blog on Pinterest. For your blog, Pinterest will function as an external referrer.

You can also find immensely inspiring posts on Pinterest and get recognition for your special skills. Additionally, it provides a way for people to meet new friends and benefit from a collective pool of human and social capital. In essence, Pinterest is widely successful in allowing people to plan journeys, design projects, collect ideas, plan an event, and to make wish lists.

Pinterest can be used for fun and for building a business as discussed in a later chapter.

CHAPTER 2

Create an Account

Joining Pinterest is a simple process after which you can connect with millions of people and share ideas easily. The main motivation behind joining Pinterest is that, unlike other forms of social media, the environment on Pinterest is very productive and lively because it offers a wide scale optimistic and resourceful exchange of ideas, based on people's experiences. The diversity of innovative themes on Pinterest enables it to enjoy unparalleled admiration in many circles.

You can easily join Pinterest by accessing their website and clicking on: Join Pinterest.

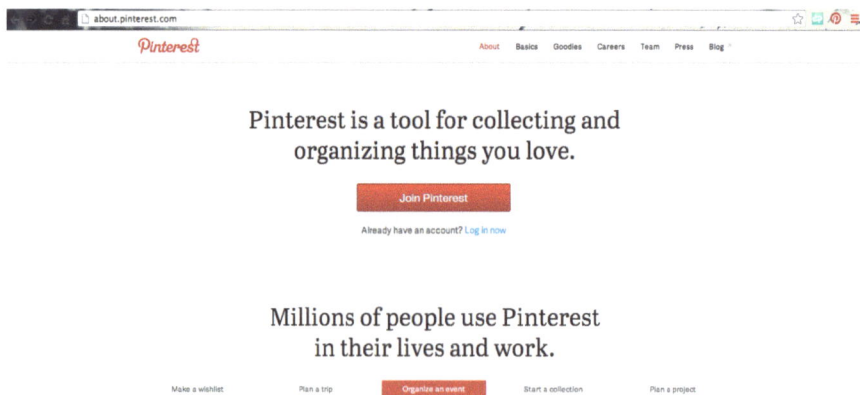

After clicking on this you will be redirected to a page which asks you to join either through your existing Facebook account, Twitter or your email address.

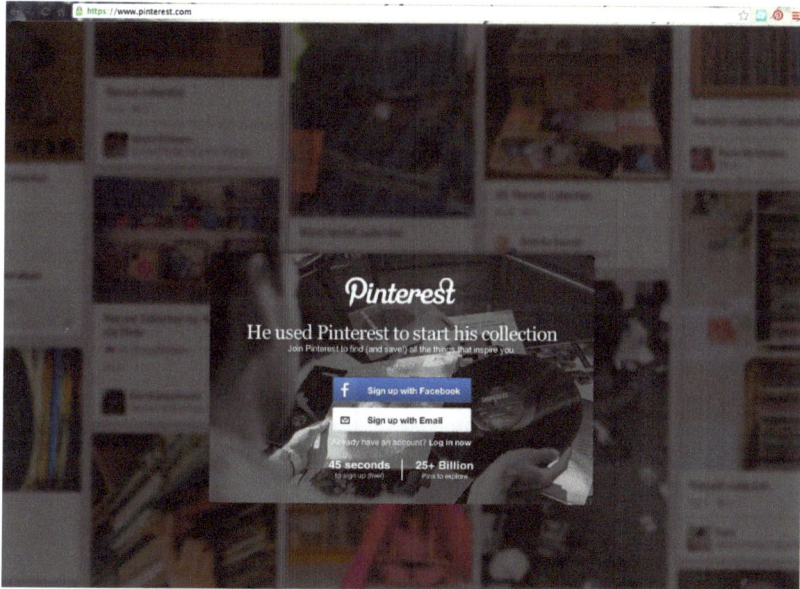

Pinterest offers businesses a chance to have accounts to promote their offerings. It may be advantageous to keep personal and business accounts separate.

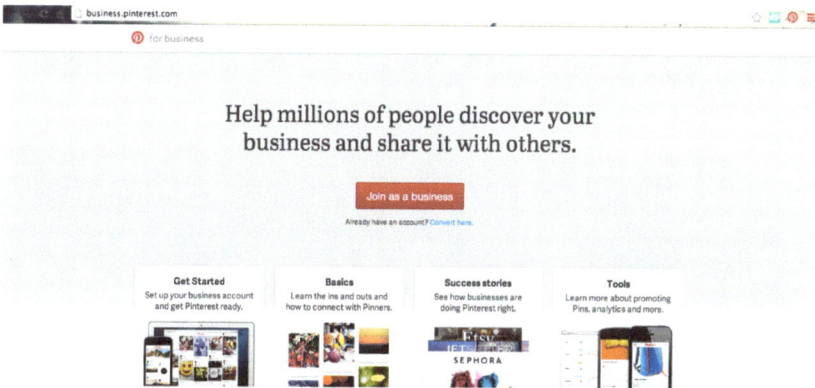

Signing up with Facebook

By clicking on 'Sign Up with Facebook' you will be directed to a page which asks you to confirm this action.

Click on Log In.

The App Page will appear which will authorize Pinterest to use your Facebook information for setting up the account. If you approve of this, simply click on 'Go to App'.

Create your account

Uncheck the boxes if you do not want Facebook to access this information

Follow recommended friends
Publish activity to Facebook Timeline

By creating an account, I accept Pinterest's **Terms of Service** and **Privacy Policy**.

Create Account

After this another webpage will appear, in which you will create your account by adding your personal information and you can also choose whether you want your Pinterest activity posted on your Facebook page or not.

Signing up with Your Email

If you choose to sign up with your email address, you will be shown another window in which you are required to enter your personal information in the fields. This includes your full name, email address, password, country and gender. You can also check the box if you want to personalize your experience with Pinterest based on other sites you visit.

Sign up with Email ✕

| First Name _Required_ | Last Name |

| Email Address |

| Password |

| United States ▼ |

○ Female   ○ Male

☑ Let Pinterest personalize your experience based on other sites you visit · **Learn more**

Are you a business? **Click Here**

By creating an account, I accept Pinterest's **Terms of Service** and **Privacy Policy**.

Cancel   Sign up

Creating a Business Account

If you are a business, you will be required to choose the option relevant to that. In this section you would have to add details about your enterprise.

How to increase sales using Pinterest

First, select your business type then add the Contact Name, email address, password. The Profile Info requires you to add information that will be publically available to everyone on Pinterest, which includes your business name, username, profile image, your business description and your website URL.

About | Enter a description for your profile

Website | Enter your website address | ex: http://yourwebsite.com

AGREEMENT

Terms of Service

Thank you for using Pinterest!

Pinterest's products and services are provided by Pinterest, Inc. These Business Terms of Service ("Business Terms") govern your access to and use of Pinterest's website, products, and services ("Products") for commercial purposes. Please read these Terms carefully, and contact us if you have any questions. By creating a Commercial Account, or by accessing or using our Products, you agree to be bound by these Terms and by our Privacy Policy.

1. Using Pinterest

a. Who can use Pinterest

You may use our Products only if you can form a binding contract with Pinterest, and only in compliance with these Terms and all applicable laws. When you create your Pinterest account, you must provide us with accurate and complete information. Any use or access by anyone under the age of 13 is prohibited. If you open an account on behalf of a company,

Accept Terms | ☐ I agree to the Business Terms of Service and Privacy Policy

After this, you will have to accept the Terms of Service and click on Create Account.

Following these steps, your Personal or Business account will be created on Pinterest and you will receive a confirmatory email on your email address. Once you start using Pinterest, getting involved in trends is extremely intuitive and natural. You can begin by installing the Pin It button onto your web browser so that you can directly pin ideas from different websites on to your pin board. Pinterest will ask you to choose from some basic things that interest you so that you can get started.

Click a few things you like:

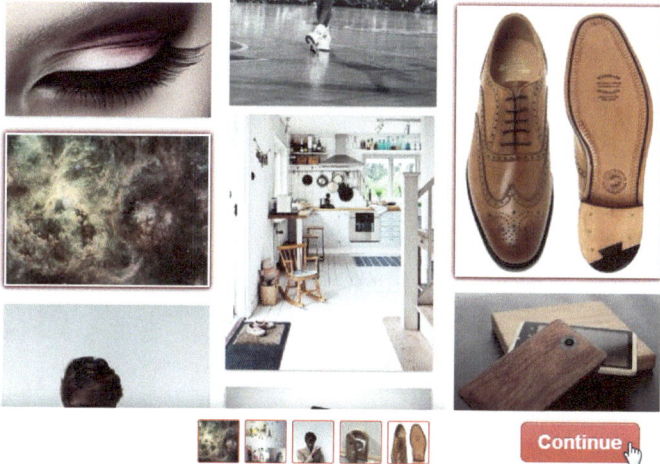

After clicking Continue, your account is ready for use; you should start browsing boards of other people who share your interests or have ideas which might interest you. You can start following them to receive updates about what they pin.

There are two ways to follow: either you can follow all the boards or another person or you can follow only the boards which interest you. For increasing your interaction base you should follow all boards.

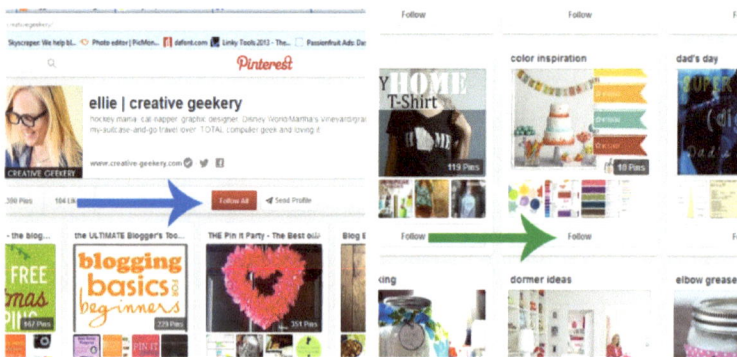

CHAPTER 3

Set Up a Personal Profile

The best feature of social media websites like Pinterest is that they allow users to personalize their experience and actively create their online personas by sharing information and connecting with like-minded people.

Each person brings his or her own unique personality and interests to Pinterest and makes it a platform filled with a volley of incomparable and unusual ideas. In this way Pinterest also becomes a great tool for visual learning, since it teaches people in a stepwise way to do things like make recipes, design items, complete different arts and crafts projects and collect items and document dreams.

Connect to Facebook or Twitter

Before you can share Pins on Facebook or Twitter, you'll need to connect your Pinterest profile to those accounts.

1. Click your name in the top right corner of Pinterest then click **Settings**
2. Switch **Login with Facebook** or **Login with Twitter** to Yes
3. Click **Save Settings**

Share Pins on Facebook

Automatically share all your Pins on Facebook:

1. Click your name at the top of Pinterest then click Settings
2. Switch Link to Timeline to Yes
3. Click Save Settings

Social Networks

f Connected **https://www.facebook.com/clarettataylorpam**

Log in with Facebook	Yes	Use your Facebook account to log in
Link to Timeline	No	Post your activity to Timeline

Connected **http://twitter.com/TaylorPamFA**

Log in with Twitter	Yes	Use your Twitter account to log in

8+ Not connected to Google+

Connect with Google+	No	Connect to Google+

M Connected to Gmail

Connect with Gmail	Yes	Connect to Gmail

Y! Not connected to Yahoo

Connect with Yahoo	No	Connect to Yahoo

Deactivate Account   Cancel   Save Settings

Manually share a Pin on Facebook or Twitter:
1. Click on a Pin to see it close up and click the **Share** icon
2. Select **Facebook** or **Twitter**
3. If you haven't connected your Facebook or Twitter, you'll see a prompt to connect it to Pinterest
4. Click **Share** for Facebook or **Tweet** for Twitter

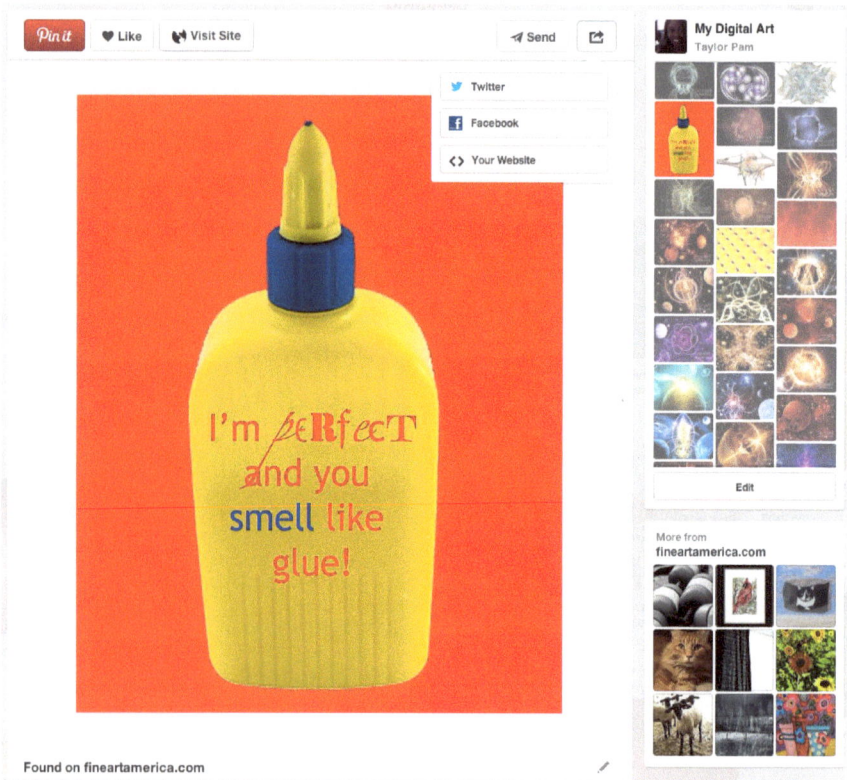

Check your Facebook settings:

If you hid Pinterest activity on Facebook, you'll need to update your settings to show these stories again:

Go to the Pinterest app on Facebook (the address will look like: facebook.com/YOURUSERNAME/app_pinterestapp)

1. Click **Activity Log** at the top right corner
2. Click the second icon next to **This app can post on your behalf to:**
3. Make sure all the options are checked

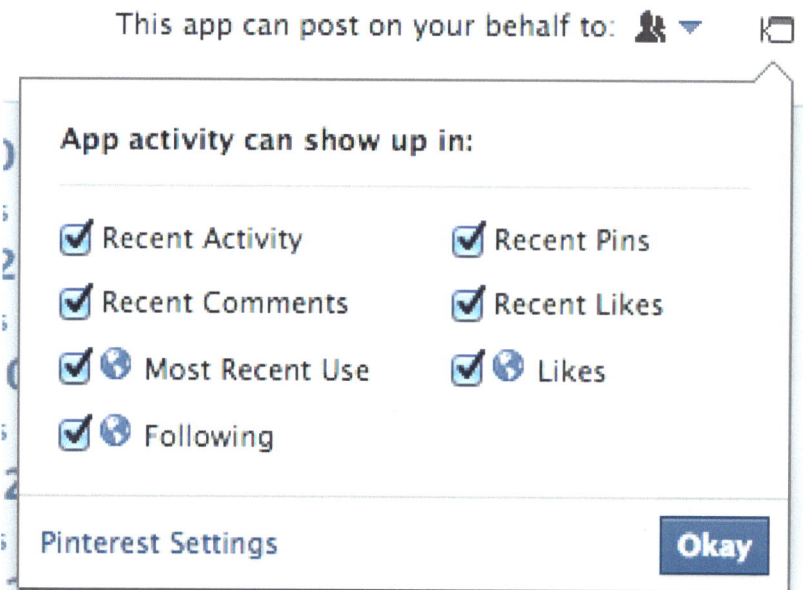

This app can post on your behalf to:

App activity can show up in:

☑ Recent Activity   ☑ Recent Pins

☑ Recent Comments   ☑ Recent Likes

☑ 🌐 Most Recent Use   ☑ 🌐 Likes

☑ 🌐 Following

Pinterest Settings   **Okay**

Show Pinterest stories on Timeline:
If you'd like, you can force Pinterest stories to show on your Timeline.

Go to your Facebook profile
1. Click **Activity Log** at the top right of your profile
2. Find a Pinterest story and click on the pencil icon
3. Choose **Shown on Timeline** to force the story to show up on your profile

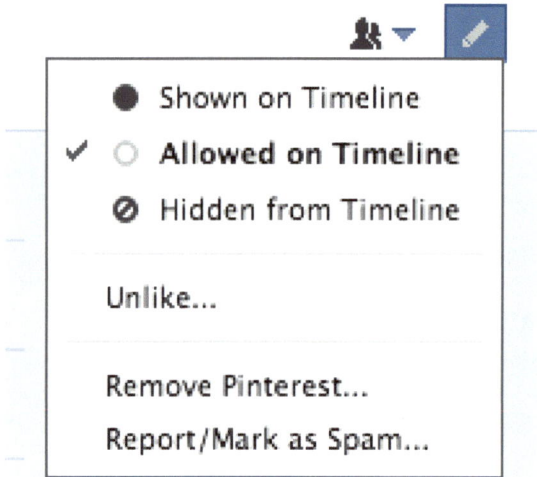

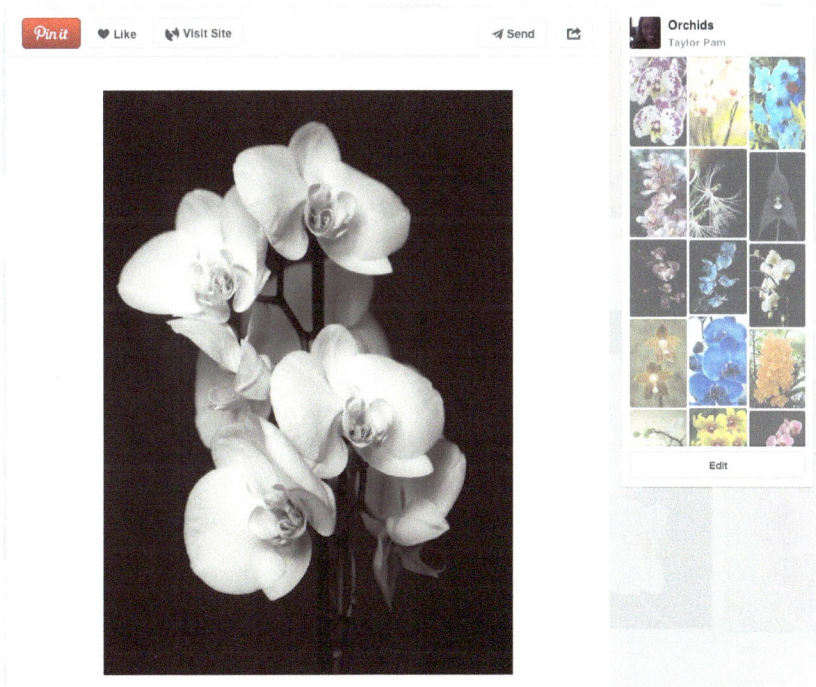

By re-pinning posts and creating your own boards you are defining your personality, hobbies and interests and dreams. At the same time it is very important to stay connected on Pinterest and to receive the right recognition for your own work. This can be made possible by increasing the appeal of your profile so that more people will follow your boards and your original ideas will gain the right audience.

There are a few steps you can follow to increase your popularity on Pinterest.

1. Categorize Boards: Boards are the means through which you can effectively categorize the content you post. You should always find a board in which you can pin items because this will enable people to

view your content when they conduct a category wise search. For instance, if you have designed homemade jewelry and you haven't pinned it in the Arts and Crafts or Jewelry category then people who search for these categories only, might never come across your work. Click 'Edit' on a specific board and add it to the most relevant category.

2. Describe your Board: Telling viewers about the content and main theme of your board helps them refine their search and saves their time. It can also help you give them valuable information about the pinned posts. If you post original content, it is extremely important to add a description and improve your brand image.

3. Personalize Boards: Another way to attract other users is to personalize your board by changing the cover image which appears on each board. Make sure that the cover picture represents the board and your personality and is sufficiently attractive for new users. A minor caveat is that the cover choice has to be made every time you pin something new.

4. Provide Information about Yourself: In the text box of your profile you should enter general details about yourself and even add links of your profiles on other social media websites so that people with shared interests or backgrounds can easily follow you. This will also give a personal and credible element to

your work because people will be able to relate to you as a person.

5. Rearrange: Place your best boards on top of the page so that people can easily see it. You can select the boards which are more popular and attractive, in order to make them visible to new audiences.

6. Synchronize your Profiles: Connecting your Facebook or Twitter to your Pinterest account may also get you more followers.

Personalizing your Pinterest will allow you to connect with new and interesting people easily.

CHAPTER 4

Set Up a Business Profile

Pinterest also offers great scope for new and established businesses to widen their audience and to advertise their brand. Pinterest provides a large pool of users for businesses which are interested in mass marketing online. Unlike other websites Pinterest provides a range of interests and a very clearly well-defined audience which can be easily targeted leading to a high rate of returns for online businesses.

Keep Your Customers First

As a business your primary aim should be about finding out what your users prefer by looking at your web analytics. These will guide you about which pins have the maximum number of shares, how many people you reach, the number of impressions made and so on. Use this information to customize your pins and directly approach your potential customers.

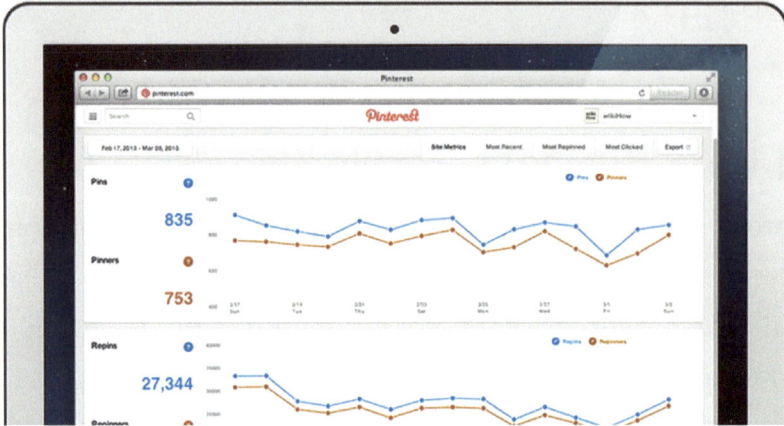

Make Your Boards Attractive

The way you will reach your customers is through the items pinned in your boards. Therefore try to customize your board according your products, different trends, or any other type of theme which makes navigation easy for new users. As mentioned earlier the cover photos of your boards make the first impression and should be sufficiently attractive. For instance, the board of Global Realty & Investment Corp about Apartments for Rent is very attractive:

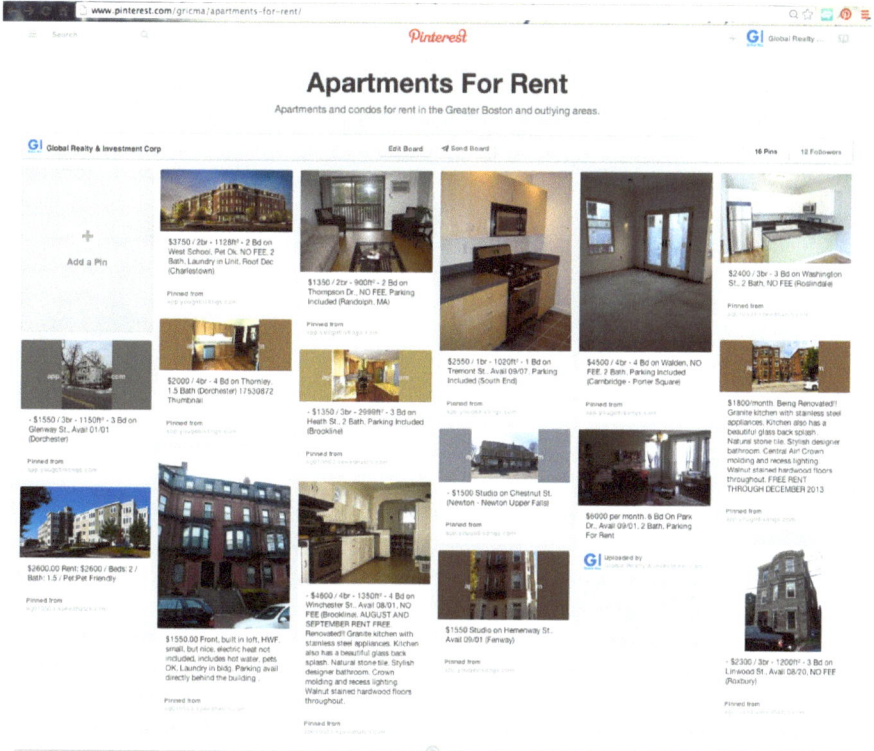

Connect

The problem with most mass marketing techniques is that they are geared towards selling the product only and not towards building a relationship with the customer. In Pinterest you can easily develop the bond between consumers and producers by telling them about the inspirations, stories, or background of your business or products. For instance you could tell them about the way a product design was conceived or the history of the founders of the business; if you connect with potential users in this way it will help humanize your business.

Originality

The right combination of originality and creativity is a surefire recipe for success on Pinterest. You need to haul in your creative genius and brainstorm about various ideas, themes and subjects about which you can pin posts and create content.

Share

Sharing your website links and the links to your Facebook profile will help users connect with you on more than one platform. You should also share your pinned posts on your website in order to drive traffic towards your business and to increase the popularity of your brand.

Add the Pin Button

Another very crucial thing for businesses is to add the Pin It button on their website so that users who are on Pinterest can easily pin the content from the website to their own boards.

To add the Pin It button to a website, go to the widget builder on the Pinterest website.

http://business.pinterest.com/widget-builder/#do_pin_it_button

It's extremely simple to configure your button. The first step is to fill out the form press the BUILD IT button, copy the resulting HTML and paste the code where you want the button to be on the website.

Widget builder

Add a Pinterest button or widget to your website. You can also add a Pin It button to your iOS or Android app.

| Pin It Button | Follow Button | Pin Widget | Profile Widget | Board Widget |

Pin It button: Invite people to Pin things from your website.

Button Type:	One Image · Any Image · Image Hover
Appearance:	Small ▾ Rectangular ▾ Gray ▾ English ▾
Show Pin Count:	Above the Button ▾
URL:	http://www.flickr.com/photos/kentbrew/6851755809/
Image:	http://farm8.staticflickr.com/7027/6851755809_df5b2051c9_z.jpg
Description:	Next stop: Pinterest

Build It!

Claretta T. Pam

CHAPTER 5

Making 'Boards'

Now that you are familiar with the absolute basics of Pinterest, its time you started learning how to use the website. The first things you will need to learn about are Pinterest 'boards'. In this section, we will discuss everything there is to Pinterest boards, how to use them, how to optimize them for internet searches and how to organize them.

What is a Board?

No doubt you will be familiar with pin boards. These are made of cork and are typically found in offices or study rooms and have posters, advertisements, memos, timetables and general pieces of infotainment pinned to them. Anyone who passes by the board can see the things that are pinned to it.

Now imagine that same physical pin board were converted into an online board. All the pins remained until you delete them, and all your friends and acquaintances could see what you have pinned to it. This is essentially what a Pinterest board is: an online pin board.

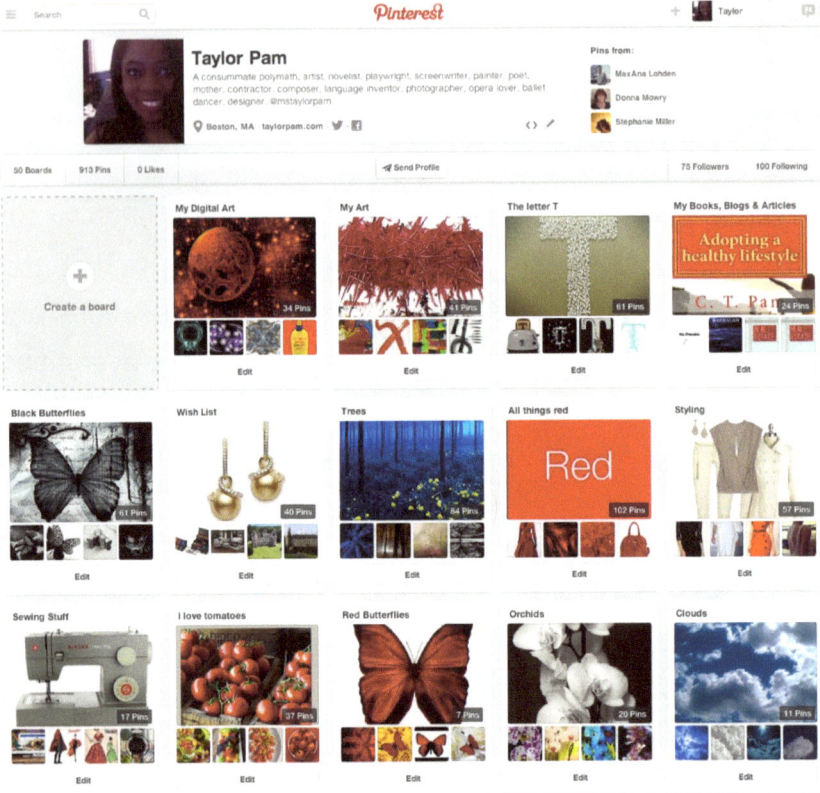

As you might imagine, unlike an actual pin board, there are an infinite number of things, which you can 'pin' to an online board like the one you get with Pinterest. This is, in fact, the beauty of a Pinterest board. Any content that you find appealing or attractive can be pinned to your Pinterest board. Music, videos, pictures, web links and plain text are just some of the most popular things which Pinterest users like to pin. But how do you go about making a board on Pinterest?

How to make a Board

Your main Pinterest page will have a 'Add +' button in the upper right-hand corner. Click on it and then give your board a name and description. Pinterest also offers a whole list of board categories from which you can choose. This includes Education, Food & Drink, Home Décor, Illustrations and Posters, and Gardening among several others.

Once you have created your profile, you should add Pin It buttons to your browser. These will allow to you pin whatever you like on the internet directly onto your Pinterest boards. You can also specify types of boards such as secret boards (which will be discussed in detail in a later chapter) and joint boards.

Pinterest Categories

Pinterest
Categories

Animals
Architecture
Art
Cars & Motorcycles
Celebrities
Design
DIY & Crafts

Education
Film, Music & Books
Food & Drink
Gardening
Geek
Hair & Beauty
Health & Fitness
History
Holidays & Events
Home Decor
Humor
Illustrations & Posters
Kids

Men's Fashion
Outdoors
Photography
Products
Quotes
Science & Nature
Sports
Tattoos
Technology
Travel
Weddings
Women's Fashion
Other

Joint Boards

Joint boards are shared boards, and they allow you select other pinners who can add their own content to them. However, since you have created the board, they will not be able to change its title or category.

With your board created, you can start to enjoy the wonders of Pinterest! Pin your favorite items to your boards and share them with others. Collect and organize your pins according to their boards, to make it easy for your followers to find your content.

You can also follow other people's boards and pin anything you like from them. This way your popularity on Pinterest will spread, as well your following. Remember that your Pinterest boards are all about you, so be original and express yourself in a creative and appealing fashion.

Creative Board Ideas

Let's take a look at some creative ideas for Pinterest boards, which will surely make you very popular. Of course, these are just some popular ideas, and you can be as creative as you like.

1. **Fashion:** The fashion industry is booming like never before and designer clothes, shoes and accessories have

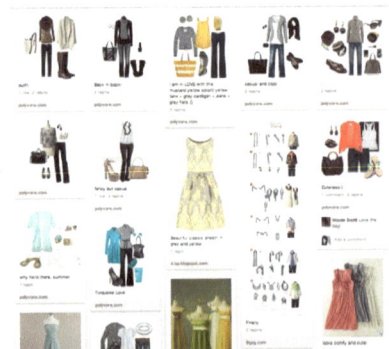

become synonymous with elements of popular culture. Making a board where you pin all your favorite fashion related items such as photos of dresses, shoes and handbags (among other things) is an excellent way to get a lot of repins and followers.

2. **Recipes and food:** These are one of the most popular board types on Pinterest. Whether you are an aspiring chef or already a master in the kitchen, one great way to create a portfolio for your recipes is to get them onto a Pinterest board. Those who follow you will definitely try them out and leave comments.

3. **Interior Décor:** Everyone loves a beautiful home. More than that, people like looking at pictures of beautiful home interiors. There is just something about a new, clean and crisp interior that makes people feel perfectly comfortable. So, you could be someone who just likes looking at all things homely and beautiful, or you could be looking for reviews from some people on your own home interior ideas. Either

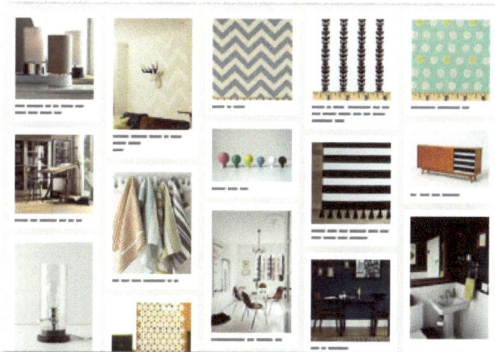

way, interior décor is a great idea for a Pinterest board.

4. **Quotations:** We all have certain words of wisdom which resonate in our minds and continue to drive our efforts and enthusiasm. They bring us up when we are down, and they make us see the bright side even when things get dark. So you could create a board with your favorite quotations pinned to it, and they might just make someone's day!

5. **Books:** Books are our favorite companions. They are the best of listeners and the most patient of teachers. If you are one of those people who simply cannot spend a minute of idleness without grasping your nearest novel, self-help book or monthly digest, then perhaps you could create a board of your favorite books. You will definitely attract like-minded book lovers.

6. **Hair, Beauty and Make-up:** The popularity of this board type is perhaps second only to fashion. The latest hairstyles have a tendency to become the image defining aspects of modern fashion, and make-up accessories such as lipsticks, eyeliners, mascaras and hair colors always compliment them. You could pin photos of whichever hairstyle is turning

heads and techniques on how to get that style. You could also pin photos of eye-catching make-up, and some video demonstrations of how to apply them.

7. **Celebrities:** Actors and singers have always had the world's attention. Perhaps there is someone among them who catches your attention quite often! You could pin photos of your favorite movie stars, their fashion and clothing styles, their lifestyle or maybe just some generic photos of them. Your board will become very popular when you find people who like them as much as you do.

8. **Places:** Travel destinations are great way to share your dream vacations. Pinterest will give you an opportunity to travel without leaving the comfort of your home.

9. **Architecture:** Buildings all over the world are a great way to show the detail in beautiful structures. Grand staircases and pillars are just the beginning of a world journey. You can pin photos of skyscrapers or historic sites.

5 Ways to Use Secret Boards

We first mentioned secret boards at the beginning of this section. Now let's take a closer look at them. Essentially, Pinterest allows you to create a special type of board, known as a secret board, the content visibility for which you can completely control. So you can keep the content of your secret board hidden from the public if you want to do so.

What's a secret board?

A secret board is only visible to you and to anyone you invite to it.

When you add a Pin to a secret board, it won't show up anywhere else on Pinterest — not in the category sections, anyone's search results, your followers' home feed, your own home feed, or even Pins or activity pages on your profile.

Your secret boards are at the bottom of your profile. Just scroll down to see them.

🔒 **Keep some boards secret** — only you (and people you invite) can see these boards. **Learn more**

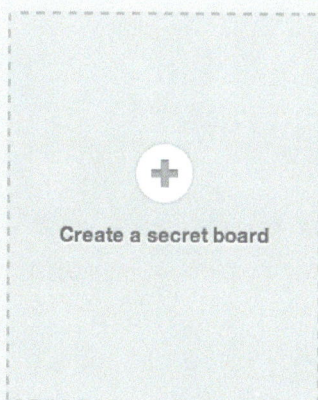

Create a secret board

Create a Board   ✕

Name	Business Ideas

Description	Business ideas to be launched in 2020

Category	Technology ⬍

Add a map?	No

Keep it secret?	Yes	Learn more

Cancel   **Create Board**

Add a secret board

1. Click your name at the top of Pinterest then click **Your Boards.**
2. Scroll to the bottom of your boards.
3. Click **Create a Secret Board.**
4. Choose a name and category for your board. The secret setting will already be set to Yes – this means your board is secret.

   Note: Any time you're adding a new board, you can switch the secret setting to Yes to make it a secret board. But you can't make an existing public board secret.

How many secret boards can I have?

Current Limits:

- Boards: 350

- Pins: 100,000

- Likes: 100,000

- All boards that you create will count towards the 350-board limit - including secret boards. If you have more creating to do, it is suggested that you create another Pinterest account with a new email address.

- There's no limit on the number of secret boards you can *participate* on – if you accept an invite to a secret board, it won't count against the board limit.

Make a secret board public

If you want to make a secret board public (remember, this can't be undone!):

1. Go to the board and click **Edit**
2. Turn the secret setting from Yes to **No**
3. **Save Changes** and confirm that you want to make the board public

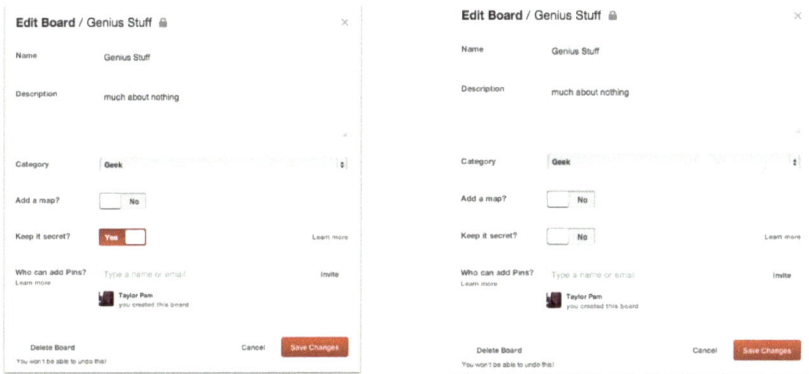

Although this obviates the entire purpose of your Pinterest profile, there are several reasons why you might want to create a secret board. Here, we will take a look at 5 ways in which you could use secret boards on Pinterest.

1. **Work on a project:** This is an excellent way to use a secret board. Since Pinterest is an immensely visual-oriented website, there are endless ways in which

you could share ideas with others. So if you are working on a specific project, the details of which you would rather keep a secret, then you could brainstorm about it with your colleagues on your secret board. You can discuss design ideas for new products, new techniques for creative work, and even photos and videos which you are editing.

2. **Conduct market intelligence and research:** If you are a business, then you will want to keep an eye on your competition. A secret board is a great way to do this. You can pin content from your competing businesses boards onto it, without them knowing. Of course, if you have added other people to your secret board, then you can discuss things on it about the new products being introduced by other businesses. You could also analyze content which general Pinterest users have pinned, and which draws a lot of web traffic to their boards and website. Get inspired, and then make your own content!

3. **Create anticipation for a new product:** If you have a large enough gathering of followers, and a line of successful products associated with your brand name, then you have won yourself the right to create anticipation for your newest product. Since, a secret board allows you to add content before making it public, you could get some hype going about your

new product by creating an attractive board icon and not giving away too many details. Then, when the time is right, and enough content is on the board, open it to the public.

4. **Plan surprise events:** You could be planning a surprise birthday party for someone, and not wanting them to find out about it. Creating a secret board will allow you to share ideas, themes, cake recipes, gift ideas and locations with other people who may also be planning the party. You could do the same if you were planning something like an office Christmas party.

5. **Maintain your privacy:** This is perhaps the most obvious use of a Pinterest secret board. Sometimes, you just want to organize your thoughts and content. Pinterest allows you to do that without alerting other people. If there is an article that you do not others to read, a web-link you do not want them to visit, or a photo you do not want them to see, you could pin it to your secret board without them noticing.

Although the usage of Pinterest secret boards can undoubtedly lead to inappropriate content making its way onto the internet, Pinterest has assured users that it will monitor the content on these boards and keep an eye out for anything objectionable.

How to Search Optimize your Boards

If you truly want to embrace popularity through Pinterest, then the way to go about it is to use search engine optimization (SEO). This is a technique used by bloggers, article writers, academics and contributors to general databases on the internet, which allows their content to turn up more frequently on search engine results.

Although Pinterest users have the ability to follow specific

pins, the website is encouraging users also to follow boards as well. Therefore, search optimizing your boards has become very important. Here, we will take a look at some ways in which you can search optimize your Pinterest boards.

1. **Make Use of Keywords:** This is arguably the most important thing when it comes to search optimizing your boards. In fact, this is the key when it comes to using SEO for any sort of content which you want discovered on the internet. Keywords are the words

that search engines use to find relevant results. When a person types something into the search bar, Pinterest (or a search engine like Google) finds content with words which match the typed text. So use sensible keywords, which accurately but concisely describe the content, because they are more likely to be searched for.

2. **Gather a lot of Followers:** Although this may sound slightly obvious, but if you have more followers for your existing boards, then it is also more likely to turn up in Pinterest search results. Although the number of pins also matters, but if the board has a lot of followers, i.e. in the 10,000 to 40,000 range, then it will definitely be among the first search result names which turn up. The way to get more followers is to pin good quality content on a regular basis.

3. **Pin Good Quality Content in Large Numbers:** This is Pinterest Popularity 101. There is nothing which plays a more crucial part in getting you a lot of followers than the quality of your content. Obviously, it is hard to get a heap of excellent quality content, but you should aim to pin your best photos, videos, music, web-links, quotes etc. on your boards. Make sure your content is relevant to your theme, and try to be original. The number of pins also matters, since the more pins you have, the larger a user base

you will appeal to and thus the more followers you will attract.

4. **Follow Other People:** One excellent way of getting noticed is if you follow other people's boards, which pique your interest. Again, only follow the ones specific to your likes, and comment on pins which you really like. Repin from other people's boards, as well. Eventually you will start to get noticed. Your name and the popularity of your boards will also spread. You will get more followers and your board will begin showing up in search results.

5. **Segment your Boards:** Instead of creating one board which has all your favorite recipes, why not make a separate one for breakfast recipes, one for lunch recipes, another for dinner and one for desserts? That is just one example of board segmenting. This technique will allow you to target more specific audiences, and your likelihood of turning up in search results will also increase.

The Pinterest Search Board function allows you (or any other user) to find the board of your choice. It displays lots of suggestions according to number of followers, number of pins and keywords. So, if you want your boards to be discovered, make sure you have search optimized them for Pinterest.

Tips for Organizing Boards

Your boards work best to attract followers when they are arranged properly. Here, we will discuss some techniques which you could use to organize your boards in order to

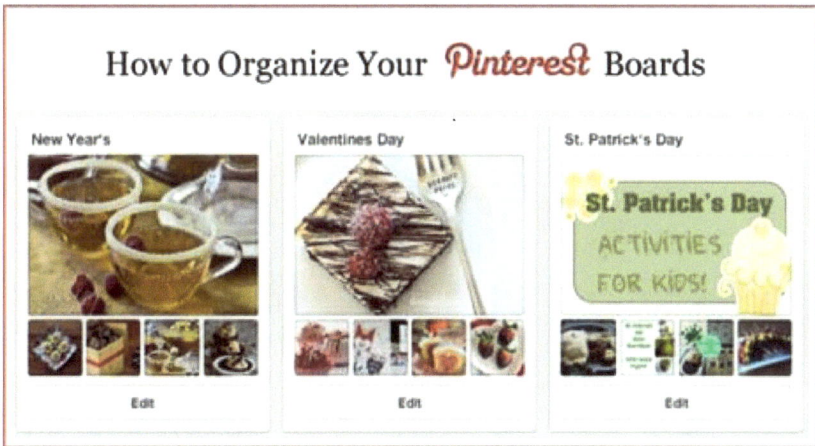

make them more visually pleasing for those who visit your profile.

1. **Display your Best Content in the Center:** Aesthetically speaking, the boards that you place in the top-center of your page are the ones that first catch viewer's attentions. Make sure you place your best boards in this position. The first two rows should also contain some of your best and most recent boards, which should be arranged chronologically and also according to subject. If you arrange your boards perfectly, they will tell a great story about you and your work!

2. **Make Attractive Board Covers:** Again, this point emphasizes the importance of showing your best work. Whichever is your best image of the board should ideally be the cover for that particular board, and it should be properly aligned so that it shows perfectly. Keep changing your cover photos so that they do not become stagnant.

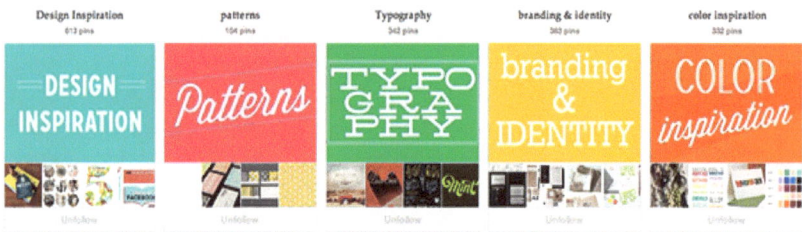

3. **Clean your Boards:** Every now and then, you should try and clean up your boards so that they do not contain any content that has been pinned for too long. Keep your items fresh and up-to-date and delete older ones which have few repins. This will show your followers you actually care about what you pin, and that you keep in touch with the latest trends.

4. **Use Proper Descriptions and Categories:** When you create a new board, Pinterest allows you to specify a category to it. Make sure that whatever category you select matches the type of content you wish to pin to the board. Also, add a proper, relevant

description for the board, so that your followers know its theme and content.

Once you have organized your boards in this manner, you will be quite pleased with the results. Not only will it make your page visually pleasing, but it will also help in attracting the right Pinterest audience.

CHAPTER 6

Making the Most of Pinterest

In the last section, we looked at Pinterest boards. Now, we will discuss in detail some of the strategies which relate to pinning the right content and promoting yourself, and how these relate to the number of followers you have on Pinterest. The number of Pinterest followers obviously affects your sales as a business, and thus the amount of revenue you generate.

Find More Followers

The two most important purposes of Pinterest are to allow you to express yourself in a creative and original manner, and to allow other people to see your work and appreciate your method of expression. After all, Pinterest is a social networking site, so your goal would be to gather as many followers as you can. Here are some tips on how to do that.

1. **Use the Pinterest Follow Button:** The follow button is very useful in getting followers if your website receives a lot of visitors. You can install the button in

a corner of the webpage, and when visitors click on it, they will be directed to your Pinterest page. Make sure you place the button somewhere it can be clearly seen, and use a custom image for the icon if you really want to make a good impression.

2. **Use the Profile Widget:** This is slightly more attractive than the Pinterest Follow Button. Though both perform the same function i.e. diverting web-traffic from your website to your Pinterest page, the Profile Widget (being much larger in size) also allows your website visitors to see up to 30 of your latest pins. You have the option of creating a custom widget, so be sure to use it.

3. **Share lots of Pins:** You may have great content, but unless you take an interest in others people's content as well, your popularity will never really grow. So when you share other people's pins which you really like, they will show up on your page and your followers will be able to see them. Pin good quality images, but at the same time try and improve your own content as well.

4. **Comment on the Most Popular Content:** Take a look at the Pinterest 'Popular' section and you will find items that have been pinned, re-pinned and commented on the most. Become a part of all those

who appreciate this work, and leave meaningful and insightful comments. This is a great way to get your own boards noticed.

5. **Associate you Social Networking Accounts:** If you use Facebook and/or Twitter then try and associate them with your Pinterest account. This is an excellent way to channel your Facebook friends and Twitter followers to your Pinterest page, and get them to notice your work. Your Pinterest account will allow you to find and add any of your contacts from other social networking sites. You could also tweet your pins on Twitter, or post them as part of your status updates on Facebook.

6. **Promote Specific Boards**: People are more likely to follow your specific boards rather than your entire account. Use this to your advantage. Promote the boards which you think showcase your best work, on specific

subjects rather than just miscellaneous content. By targeting a specific audience, you are more likely to gather a large number of followers.

7. **Contribute to Other People's Boards:** The principle is the same as that when you comment on popular content; find interesting content on others peoples boards, and comment on it. If you provide meaningful comments and pin interesting items then you will surely be noticed. Try to target those boards which have a lot of followers to improve your chances of making new followers.

8. **Follow Other Pinterest Users:** If you want to be followed, then follow others. That is a golden rule for Pinterest, and one that you must always keep in mind. People appreciate it when you follow them, and they will follow you back. You can do the same for them. To keep your content focused around a particular theme, follow those who have interests similar to yours.

9. **Run a Pinterest Contest:** This is a great follower-garnering tool if you are an up-and-coming business. You can start a Pinterest contest where anyone who is interested in participating must follow your page and repin a number of pins.

Top 4 activities for a Pinterest contest

1. Identify what you want to achieve. A) email addresses B) page likes or c) increase in visitors
2. How will you capture this info? A) Google form, b) blog post, c)pin comment
3. Require that a FOLLOW on your Pinterest and/or other social media site is required and provide the URLs as needed.
4. Capture the email of the entrant via Google form or pin comment.

10. **Keep your Followers Satisfied:** Your followers follow you for one reason only: They like your content and ideas. Therefore, try and regularly update your content to show your followers that you maintain an active and vibrant Pinterest presence, and upload pins at regularly spaced intervals instead of all at once. Try to stick to a specific topic for a particular set of followers. Remember, they are following the board because they like that specific theme.

Gathering Pinterest followers is a slow process and you need to be patient. Even after you have followed the above mentioned strategies, it will take some time before web-traffic begins to flood your Pinterest page, so do not lose hope. Keep pinning quality content and continue to network with others, and your popularity will grow.

Make it Part of Your Social Media Practice

The essence of most social media websites revolves around the fact that they are used a lot. Facebook, Instagram and Twitter particularly, allow users to provide their followers with up-to-the-minute updates on the latest happenings in their personal and professional lives. The idea behind Pinterest is not too different from this, either.

While Facebook and Twitter have a primarily textual mode of communication between different users, Pinterest is more visual oriented. The true purpose of Pinterest can only be fulfilled, and its true power realized, only when you begin to use it regularly and effectively.

This does not mean that you should constantly flood your followers news feeds with meaningless updates, but rather that you take the time out of your schedule to keep an eye on the relevance of your content, and the recent activity of your followers. Indeed, when your followers begin to notice your activity starting to diminish, they will stop following you. Your boards could lose popularity, and if left unchecked, they may disappear into the furthest reaches of Pinterest void!

Therefore, keep your content fresh and interesting. Make sure you identify the latest trends in popular culture, fashion and social media in your work, and communicate your thoughts and ideas about them in a pleasing and creative manner. Also, remember to follow other people and comment on their items if you want to gather a good number of followers.

As a business, you should always make sure your image is promoted in the best of ways. Give your boards interesting and eye-catching covers, and update them regularly. Use Pinterest Follow Buttons to redirect web-traffic from your business website to your Pinterest page. Make your Pinterest page a hub for discussions on the latest and most talked about topics in your particular field. Create a portfolio-like board for your best work so that it is noticed immediately by your followers.

Stick to Your Niche

A lot of new Pinterest users make the mistake of pinning hundreds of items to their boards. Although the larger number of items you have the more chance you have of attracting followers, you should aim at targeting specific audiences using a very definite set of themes for your Pinterest boards. In this way, you will get dedicated followers who are more likely to stay with you for a longer time.

If you are a business, you should try and focus on promoting your products and any ideas which are pertinent to your specific field. Create boards which highlight the key features of your latest products, and learn to segment them according to their genres. You could also pin items from other boards but they should complement your work in some way.

The importance of focusing your work lies in what Pinterest users perceive as dedication. When they see someone who strictly uploads cooking recipes, they will immediately think he or she is the expert in that particular field. So, gradually the relevant web-traffic will be directed towards your boards. You will get a chance to make followers who share your interests, and can provide you with meaningful insight.

Quality over Quantity

This concept is the backbone of all business ideas. Sometimes, it may seem like a platitude. For instance, if car manufacturers are targeting the masses, then they will probably want to build cars in large numbers which can satisfy the needs of the proletariat, while being economical at the same time. In this case the quality of the car will probably take a hit. That, however, is an extraordinary example.

Business ideas these days are all about giving the people exactly what they want, while still not compromising on quality. The ideas need to be clean,

clear and crisp. They should appeal instantly to the targeted audience and not form a very broad following of people from a multitude of courses. So, even though the question of quantity over quality usually involves a subjective argument, as a business promoting its idea through Pinterest, your focus should be on being selective in your content. In short, focus on the quality of the content you pin, rather than how much you pin.

Billions of people use the internet each day. Of those, there are millions who use Pinterest. We all know what it is like to use social networking sites; you scroll through what hundreds of people have shared (or pinned) and if something catches your eye, it may be lucky enough to gather your attention for a few minutes before you move on.

Therefore, the single most important thing you can hope to achieve through your Pinterest page is to capture the attention of a few, very specific people, but for a longer period of time. Of course, to do that, you should try to be very selective in the things which you pin. Ask yourself questions: Who am I targeting through my pins? Is the content actually interesting enough to get their attention? Is it too long winded or meandering? Answers to these will allow you to be very careful about what you pin. Get an actual users opinion, and see what he or she thinks.

Pinterest allows you to add description to your pins. This is your golden chance to target the right viewers. Use keywords that fit the type of image or content you have pinned, so that it shows up when someone searches for it. Again, the key is to have excellent quality content with the right keywords, so that you can attract people from a select group.

If your pins are of a very general niche, then you might get lots of people seeing your page, but none will really appreciate your content. Organize your pins into Boards, so that those who are really interested can navigate through your content and find things that interest them. Follow other people who have the same interests as you and repin their pins. Again, this will show how sedulous you are about specific ideas and interests.

Eventually, other people who see your profile, pins and content, will begin to repin your pins on their pages. Continue to add relevant content and use specific words to describe it, and with time your reputation will grow. Your presence on Pinterest will become noticed by your targeted audience all over the world, and your business ideas will become eminent.

Tell a Story

Pinterest is all about what you like and what you want to show others. So why not tell people your story? Or the story of your business? After all, a picture can provoke a thousand words, and with Pinterest you can pin an infinite number of pictures! So take this opportunity to tell people everything about how your ideas came to form and how your business has matured over the years.

There are lots of stories you can tell using pictures, and although using generic pictures garnered from random internet searches would do the job, it helps create a good impression if your pictures are actual ones of your staff and employees, meetings and celebrations. Again, be selective about the stories which you tell. Not all of them will be worth telling, and only some will be good enough to get the attention of truly interested people, as discussed in the previous chapter.

Business Background Stories and Product Histories

The origin of a business idea is perhaps the most compelling and powerful story you can tell. Some are even so epic that they have been made into films. Take the story of Facebook, and how it was the brainchild of a few genius college students: through failure and adversity, they eventually made it the internet mammoth we all know it to be today.

Could that be your own story as well? Or perhaps it could be the story of a product of yours. Explain how the ideas came to you, what motivated you to come up with them and how they evolved as the product neared completion. Was it your own idea, or did you think it up when you were brainstorming with your friends or colleagues? Also tell people how the views of the business are changing with time, and how they lead to creation of newer, better products.

Personal Stories

This type of story is designed to put you, or anyone else in your team, in the spotlight. Tell a little bit about yourself. If you are running a construction company, pin of photos of yourself playing with building blocks or LEGO bricks, as a child! Show people where the motivation and drive comes from, and how old ideas have helped you become the person you are today. People will want to know things about you and your business ideas that they do not find on the company website, so give them to them.

Put your photos in chronological order, and classify them into Boards and genres. Give them interesting titles and descriptions so that your target audience can find them easily.

There are a lot of up and coming entrepreneurs and business managers out there. Not all are confident enough to share their stories on the Internet. Share tips and advice on your Pinterest page, and how your success has come through years of hard work and dedication.

CHAPTER 7

Promote Your Brand

This section is all about promoting your business through the use of Pinterest. We will take a look at the techniques and strategies you can use on Pinterest to show people the ingenuity of your ideas, and how they help you deliver the best products and services in your particular field.

Create a Resource

Not everyone will know what your business is about before they visit your Pinterest board. Some will be attracted by the keywords, descriptions and tags that you have used, and others will simply find you because they were scrolling through news feed items and updates. It is your job to educate them about your business and services. You can do this simply by turning your board into an educational resource.

The thought of using Pinterest to teach people, who probably want to enjoy, socialize with others and express themselves, may seem dull and uncreative, but there is no reason why your Pinterest board needs to look like a high school teacher's office.

Make it interesting and engaging. Add pictures that give people lots of information about you, your company/business, the products and services you offer, and how they affect the world through people who use them each day. You do not have to adopt a conventional didactic approach to educate your audience!

The whole point of creating a Pinterest board is that people can see an aspect of your business which is very different from what you promote on your website. You may be targeting a slightly different group of people through Pinterest than you would through conventional marketing techniques. The attractive visuals and graphics that people see on your Pinterest board will give a positive business image.

Upload videos and short documentaries about your products. The videos can show the products being used in the hands of ordinary people, or they could show the product manufacturing process.

It does not necessarily have to be about your product, either, but at least something related. For instance, if you have just started a construction company, you may want to pins some graphics of how the internal machinery on a crane works, or how a cement mixer works. Again, those are just examples. It is up to you to be creative and educational in a way that attracts potential clients to you.

Update your pins regularly. People will lose interest if you do not do so. Pin videos of your new products, and describe their working and benefits, before they are released. This will create anticipation among your clientele. Keep updating your educational videos, until your fans and followers begin to see you as an informative educational resource. Fans spread the word about you to their followers and repin your pins.

Go Behind the Scenes

Giving your audiences a glimpse of the behind-the-scenes workings of your company is a great way to promote your business culture and values, particularly if you are a professional in a creative field such as the arts, photography, journalism and film making.

This is a great marketing technique, since people want to know what makes a true professional tick, what inspires them to produce great work, and how they actually go about doing their work.

Use Pinterest to pin some great videos of the inner workings of your business, and to help spread the word about your business and the admirable work ethics and principles that you support. The videos could be about the general workings of your organization i.e. the sort of work that you do on a daily basis, or they could be about a particular project which you are currently undertaking.

Make the Content Rich and Informative
Your skills with a camera are not going to win you a lot of

followers and fans. Although using high quality filming equipment is important, when it comes to making behind-the-scenes business videos, you really need to wow the audience with your content. Do not throw random clips together with music playing in the background. Rather, take your viewers through an informative and in-depth look at how your company works, and do not put too much effort into beautifying it. Remember that people will move on very quickly to something else, if they are not immediately intrigued by your videos.

Clients will notice you if and only if you have conveyed through your videos the importance of your work and made it look very interesting. Talk about who you are and then move on to what it is you are shooting. Explain the project and its goals and objectives. Perhaps you could introduce some of the key staff members who are working on it. Show the audience any equipment you are using and explain how it works. At the end, you could wrap up the video with some zoomed out shots of the entire work floor.

Focus on the Best Employees

When people see just how happy your employees or colleagues are, they will surely be impressed with your leadership and management skills. Talk to a few outstanding staff members and ask them to shoot a short interview for your video.

They should talk about themselves, their educational background and how they began working for the company.

They could move on to describe their current job role and any projects which they are working on. Finally, and this is the most important part of the video, ask them to talk about the great things about working for the company. Make it sound genuine and sincere, and avoid overly generic statements.

Get a Message from the Boss

The executive of the company embodies the values, which the business promotes. He is the shining example of success according to the company's philosophy, and so a message or advice from his is extremely valuable. You could ask him to conduct a short tour of the office floor or the work floor, or perhaps describe the importance of the company's work and the current projects and initiatives, which are underway.

Make sure your content is interesting and engaging. Once you are finished, remember to always edit your videos before uploading them. Get reviews from people around you, and improve the content, if need be.

Make it Beautiful

Pinterest wants you to express yourself as beautifully as you can. You can create a smorgasbord of appealing visuals on the website with your pinned photos and videos. This is perhaps one of the most important factors you should consider, as an up-and-coming business, when you are creating your Pinterest board.

Most people will not know what your company is all about before they have seen your board, and when they do see it, aside from your content, the most obvious thing which will catch their attention will be look of your board. So it is worthwhile investing some time into making your Pinterest board look as beautiful as it can.

The first thing to do is to set a good profile picture for yourself. Make it bold and striking. Although you could use your company's logo for the picture, try and be more creative with it. If you can, try adding more color to it without completely altering its look. The picture should be easy to identify and remember for most people, so avoid using screenshots of quotations or company mottos written in very small font. If your company does not have a logo, then maybe this is the time to make one! After all, people need a symbol to associate with a brand name.

Pay attention to the images you pin, as well. You want them to be as creative and colorful as they can be. If you are an amateur photographer, for instance, it is one thing to upload and pin great portraits that you have taken, quite another to upload high quality photos of sceneries, landscapes, trees, flowers and birds. Your photos should show the beauty and creativity which you associate with your work.

Crop and resize your photos, so that they perfectly emphasize the subject. The background is obviously very important. Make sure there are no distracting items in the background which draw attention away from the subject. In bright sunlight, deliberately pull more focus towards the subject in the foreground to make it stand out.

Create timeline-like effects by putting together several photos which capture the beauty of your subject from multiple aspects. Long photos are always more aesthetically pleasing than wider photos on Pinterest, so crop those which have too many pixels in the horizontal direction. Arrange them on your board in a collage-like manner with small, long and square shaped photos geometrically coordinated with each other. Follow and repin from those people who have uploaded excellent pictures on their boards, because that will also reflect on your board.

There are some great online software and downloadable programs which you can use to make an ordinary photo look extraordinary. Some of these provide excellent effects which you can use on your photos. Do not overdo it, though, because this will make your photos look fake. You could also hire a professional photographer to take some photos for you to market your products and services.

To sum up, the look of your Pinterest board says a lot about you and your business. So make it look attractive, and you will get the followers you want.

Highlight Philanthropic Efforts

Most multinational companies these days support at least one charity or non-profit organization. For an up-and-coming business, it is a great way to show that your corporate structure is not dominated by the need to continuously generate revenue, and also that you actually care about other people in this world.

According to Lisa Benbow, Communication Director for the UK, Ireland and South Africa at Saint-Gobain:

"Companies have a responsibility to be a good corporate citizen and supporting charities is one way to help make a positive difference to the communities they are part of."

When people see a caring and compassionate side to your company's workings, it creates a sense of good will and support in the community, and they feel attached to you. They will feel more loyal to your brand and are much more likely to support you when they see that you are actively trying to become a contributing part of this world.

Although you could tie the purpose of your business to a specific charity, where a common set of interests are shared, but you could also simply support a charity which works for a cause that you are passionate about. You could also talk to your employees and see which charity the majority is interested in supporting.

You can create awareness among your employees, as well as the general Pinterest user base, by pinning photos related to causes which you support. Add suitable captions and descriptions to make them informative. For personal stories that have moved you, make sure your followers and clients learn about them as well. Pin these stories, in pictorial form, with good captions on your boards and share them with your followers.

People who visit your Pinterest boards will be able to see these photos and will admire you for your compassion. Furthermore, supporting non-profit organizations and charities is an excellent marketing strategy. When your brand name becomes associated with good will, volunteer work and noble causes, it will spread more rapidly.

Pin photos of your staff members and managers working alongside members of charitable organizations and engaging in volunteer work (such as building homes and working in shelters), and they will definitely be noticed by people. Arrange for charitable events such as marathons, food and clothes collections, silent auctions, bake sales, golf events etc. Pin good quality photos of these events on your boards. You could also make videos with employees stressing how important it is to give back the community, how much they enjoyed attending the event and how much the company is passionate about the cause itself.

The major charities and non-profit organizations all use Pinterest, now. Some of these include Oxfam, WWF and UNICEF. They pin a lot of images and videos for the purpose of raising funds, inspiring people and creating awareness. Take this as your chance to give back to the world, and spread your own brand name in the process. Follow their pages and repin from their boards. This is an excellent way to show the world how fervent your company is about pursuing noble causes.

Become a Part of Pop Culture

Popular culture has completely changed the way we see the world. With the advent of limitless social networking opportunities and ways to express yourself on the internet like never before, we have been brought closer together through the similarity in our interests and passions. Our attitudes, ideas and perspectives have changed entirely, through popular culture.

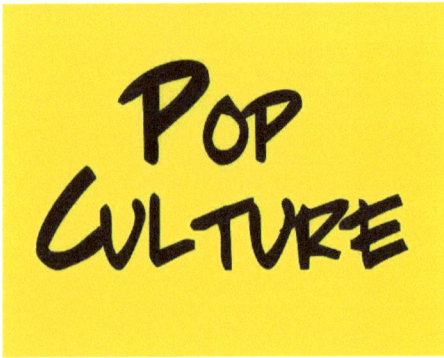

Businesses, including some of the world's largest brands, have taken full advantage of this and often use mechanisms in popular culture to reach the masses. This is particularly effective because consumers these days are a lot more receptive to the public fascinations, celebrity lifestyles and popular trends.

Conventional marketing strategies are becoming stagnant and companies are struggling to find consumers who will stay loyal for long periods of time. However, in recent times, it has been shown that the usage of pop culture in your product marketing campaigns can make you unique in the eyes of consumers, which is very hard to do in today's world. Obviously, using pop culture is trickier than it seems.

You need to be subtle, yet entertaining in your approach. By appealing to the fascination of the public, your brand name can itself become a part of the pop culture that you are utilizing. The question then becomes one of how to go about integrating pop culture into your marketing strategies. The basic idea is that you use whatever current social issues are prevalent, and associate them in a non-obvious way to your product.

For instance, when Oreo (the cookie producer) began using pop culture to their advantage, they created an image of their cookie in which the filling was reminiscent of the surface of Mars, with the Mars Rover Curiosity's tracks visible in red colored filling. Thus, wherever people spoke about the Mars Rover, they spoke about Oreos!

There is no reason you could not do the same for your products. Find the latest hot topics, or developments, and try to create a link between it and your brand name. Another great technique is to show the history and evolution of your products over the years. Oreo applied this strategy as well, and chose some of the most identifiable achievements in human history to associate their brand with. This created the impression that they had been around for a very long time, and were a trusted and reliable brand.

You need to cautious of the timing of your pop culture oriented marketing, as well. If there is a certain social conversation taking place, then you should utilize it before it becomes stagnant and no longer holds the same importance in the minds of the public.

Finally, and this is very important, you need to be slightly controversial. Topics which are talked about the most in social circles also tend to be the most controversial. With

Oreo, they created their 'Gay Pride' cookie, in support of something which they believed in and which was being debated all over the world. Thus, it became part of the global discussion and Oreo's fame grew even more.

The possibilities of using pop culture are endless in today's world. Needless to say that through Pinterest, you will be able to find some of the most talked about current issues, scandals and debates, which will allow you to craft a pop-culture oriented marketing campaign for your business and products.

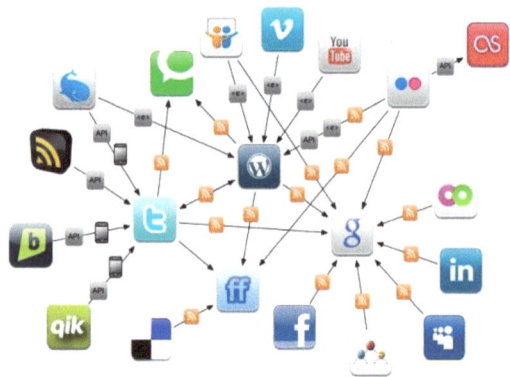

CHAPTER 8

Optimize Money-Making Potential

In this section, we will provide a much more detailed view on the tips and strategies which you could use to boost your business and earning potential on Pinterest.

Increase Web Traffic

In August 2012, Pinterest was driving more web traffic than Google, YouTube and LinkedIn combined. Although recently it has lost some of its power, it is still a mammoth for internet visitors. So, after you have spent a lot of time and effort into creating and beautifying your Pinterest board, the next thing you will want to do is to get your fair share of some of that web traffic.

As a business, you want the most web traffic to reach your board because that is how your brand name (or your name for that matter) is going to spread. Some of the ways in which you can do this are:

- **Pin your own, original content:** You could make a database of repined items from those who you really like to Pinterest, but in order to truly be influential, you need to create and pin your own content.

- **Pin videos:** Try to add some variety to your content by adding videos. We have already looked at some of the business oriented videos which you could pin on your Pinterest board, but the truth is you can be as creative as you like!

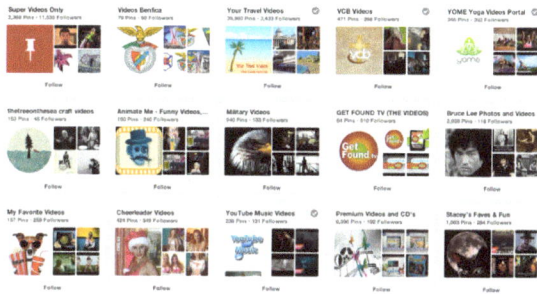

- **Distribute your pins among your boards:** Do not focus solely on one particular board; it is never a good idea to do that. You need to spread the quality pins evenly among all your boards, so that people have a reason to follow each of them, and not just one.

- **Create secret boards:** This is an excellent way to create some anticipation among your ardent followers. Use Pinterest's secret boards option to create a new board, add pins to it first, and then reveal it to the public.

- **Use Pinterest associated browser plug-ins:** You will definitely want to upload some high quality content (such as videos) at some point, on your Pinterest board. Having browser plug-ins, such as Pin-It and Pin Search, are great ways of pinning content directly from your computer to your Pinterest board.

- **Use good descriptions:** The key thing to remember is to keep your descriptions short but of good quality. People will not to read protracted testaments, but will rather be looking for to-the-point, informative content, to keep them interested and engaged. Remember to use keywords in your descriptions, as well.

- **Add Pin It buttons:** This might be one of the best ways to get your content to spread across Pinterest,

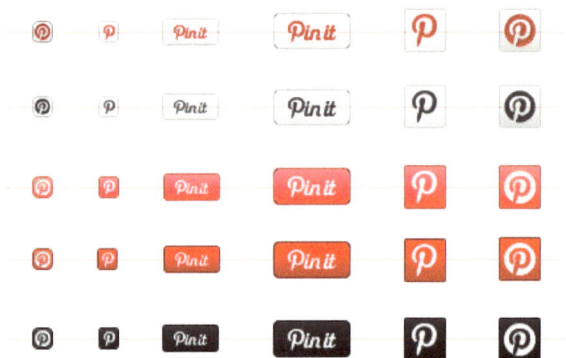

and in fact, across the internet. Use Pin It buttons, but do not use them in conjunction with other widgets, so as to avoid overcrowding your site.

- **Pin your own blog posts:** Since it is your board, do not be afraid to pin your own content. Make sure it is good quality content, and relevant to the board to which you are pinning it.

- **Verify your website:** If you are garnering a lot of followers, then it is a good idea to verify your website. This will enhance your visibility and the chances of your content showing up on search engine results, as well as allowing you to use Pinterest Analytics (discussed later).

- **Keep an eye on your analytics:** You can use software such as Google Analytics to monitor the number of people who visit your website every day/week/month.

- **Add you own descriptions:** Although a brief description of the image you pin will automatically appear when you pin it, you should try to add your own description. Be creative, but stick to the point and try not to be long-winded.

- **Make use of hashtags:** Much like Facebook and Twitter, Pinterest also allows you add hashtags in order to categorize your content. This is most effective when there are only a few categories that you want to use.

Do not become impatient if your Pinterest boards do not immediately receive a lot of followers, it takes time and effort before you will start to notice some serious web traffic being directed towards your site. Just remember to keep adding quality content.

Transform Web Traffic into Revenue

The Pinterest user base is immense. Therefore, the possibilities of harnessing that visual -oriented user base to generate revenue for your business are limitless, as well. Now that we have looked at ways of setting up your profile, making it attractive, and getting web traffic, we are going to discuss some tips for truly monetizing your Pinterest account.

With these tips you will be able to grow your mailing list, market your products and services and increase your sales.

Expand your Mailing List

You can use Pinterest to encourage potential clients to subscribe to your mailing list, and therefore increase the reach of your brand name.

- Pin images which will allow people to subscribe to your mailing list. This is useful since Pinterest has no direct way (such as a button) of allowing users to do this.

- Give people incentives to join your mailing list. These could include samples from your e-books, whitepaper statistics or short clips from training videos.
- Use creative and attractive images to get people's attention.
- Investigate techniques employed by other businesses to get people to sign-up on Pinterest.

Market your Digital Products

These would typically include games, apps or software which you think are in keeping with today's popular culture.

- Share significant statistical figures, such as satisfaction rates or popularity rates, which would encourage people to buy your product.

- Use info-graphic pages before your actual sales page, to intrigue people and keep them interested. You can then direct them to the actual sales page.
- Explain the benefits of your products. Potential customers will be interested to know how your products work and what benefits they would bring to them, so create videos which do this.
- Give a preview or demonstration of your product.

Sell Physical Products

Physical products sell very well on Pinterest, and here are some tips on how to market them:

- Show a video/photo of them being used. Make sure you use good photography/film-making equipment for this, and also provide good narration through the video.

- Get your customers positive feedback (like testimonials), or photos of them using your products and repin them on your boards, to show potential

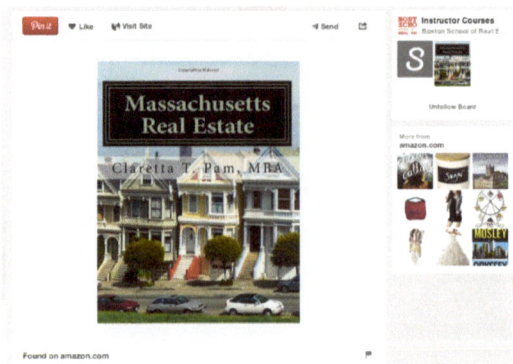

clients the level of quality and satisfaction which your service provides.

- Use Pinterest's rich pins feature.
- Provide customers with incentives such as one-time offers and discounts with your new products.

Promote your Services

If you are a service-based business, then you could use some of these tips to monetize your Pinterest account:

- Create a portfolio-like board to showcase your work. This is particularly useful if you are a professional in a creative field, such as an artist or a photographer.
- Use satisfied customer testimonials (both quotes and videos) to attract more clients.
- Share tips for amateurs in your field. For instance, if you are a photographer, you could give daily tips on how to make the best use of natural lighting while taking a photo.

THE KEY IDEA BEHIND PINTEREST IS THAT YOU ALLOW YOURSELF TO BE AS CREATIVE AS YOU CAN ABOUT YOURSELF. AS A BUSINESS, YOU NEED TO APPLY THE SAME IDEAS TO MARKET YOUR PRODUCTS EFFECTIVELY AND GAIN CLIENTS.

Claretta T. Pam

CHAPTER 9

Effective Uses of Pinterest Analytics

Pinterest Analytics is one of the best tools available out there, for marketers and businesses that are using the social media platform, to gain clients and sell products. Essentially, this feature allows you to view data and statistics related to the content which is driving the most web traffic towards your website, and which content resonates with your web audience the most.

As you can imagine, this is very handy for businesses, and here we take a look at some ways in which you can effectively use Pinterest Analytics to understand the popularity of your content.

Accessing Pinterest Analytics

As we have previously mentioned, in order to access your Pinterest Analytics, you first need to verify your website.

Edit Profile ✕

Business Name	Global Realty & Investment Corp
Picture	**GI** Global Rea [Change Picture]
Username	www.pinterest.co... gricma
About You	Global Realty & Investment Corp (GRIC) is a Boston-based, privately held real estate agency. We are available to discuss your leasing and purchasing needs.
Location	
Website	http://gric-ma.com/ [Verify Website]

Visit **Account Settings** to change your password, email address, and Facebook and Twitter settings.

[Cancel] [Save Profile]

Once you have done that, you can check the stats by clicking Analytics in the Settings menu in the upper right-hand corner of the screen.

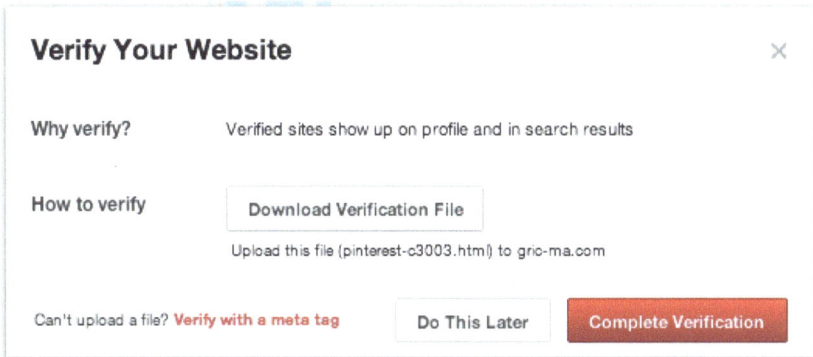

Verify Your Website   ✕

Why verify?   Verified sites show up on profile and in search results

How to verify   Download Verification File

                 Upload this file (pinterest-c3003.html) to gric-ma.com

Can't upload a file? **Verify with a meta tag**   Do This Later   **Complete Verification**

Then, from the top left-hand corner you can choose to view statistics from any time interval you specify, or any one of the pre-specified intervals. Any of the specified data types can then be exported to an MS Excel file for further analysis.

Site Metrics

This is one of the data tabs that you can choose to view from Analytics. It gives you certain notable statistics about the overall performance of your website/account.

One of the metrics that you might consider important is Pins Created From Your Website, which gives the daily average number of pins from your account. This will obviously help you determine if the content which you have pinned is interesting enough for your website visitors to pin to your boards. If you are not getting the pins which you had expected, then it may be time to add newer, more creative and visually pleasing content to your website.

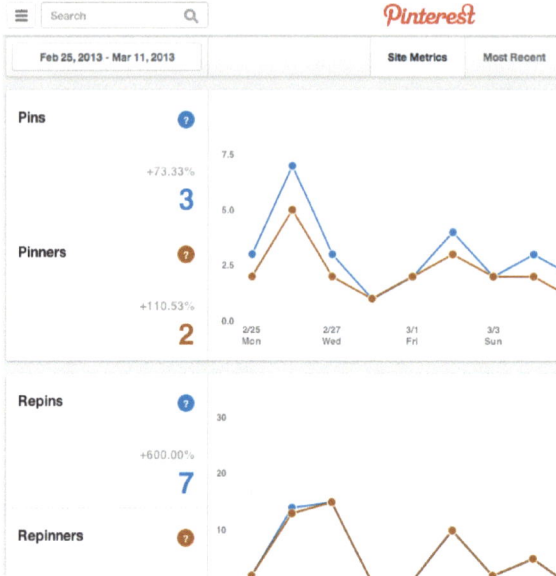

You can also look at the percentage change in pins over a certain period of time, to determine if a specific day saw an unusually high (or low) number of pins.

Repins

Repins are the most used feature on Pinterest. Users can pin items which they like on their followers pages, to their own boards. This obviously adds to the popularity of their followers, and your content will reach those who may not be in your followers list.

The Repin metric will give you the daily average number of your pins which were repined, and this will help you understand which content resonates the most with your followers, and other general Pinterest users. You can compare the Pin metric to the Repin metric to determine if your content is interesting not only to your immediate followers, but also to the general, wider Pinterest user base.

Impressions and Reach

This feature allows you to determine how many people actually saw your pins and repins, on Pinterest. After learning how many people pinned and re-pinned from your content, this is the next way to determine how successful your content is among Pinterest users.

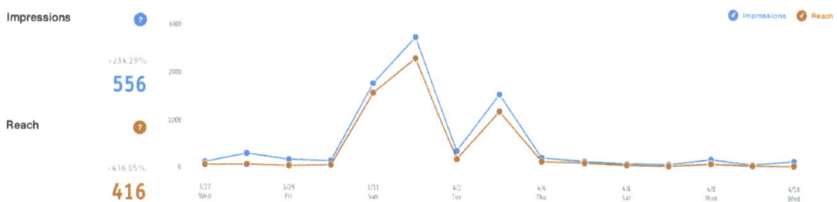

Reach allows you to see how far into the Pinterest user populace your business content has penetrated, and what its value is. For instance, if your content gets pinned and re-pinned by someone who has 30,000 followers, it has more value than the same thing being done by someone with 30 followers. Thus, Reach allows you see how much exposure your brand gained. You can also compare it with the statistic which tells you how much web traffic your content dictated to your website.

Clicks

This allows you to determine how many of your Pinterest followers were driven to your website, and thus determine how successful your overall presence is on Pinterest. The graph for Clicks gives you the number of visits to your website, and the one for Visitors give you the total number of visitors.

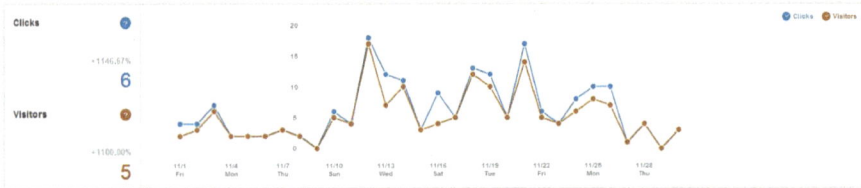

Some of your content drives engagement, while other drives traffic to your website. Comparing Clicks and Repins allows you to understand which type of response is generated by which content type. You should ensure that your content drives both activities evenly.

Most Repinned

This allows you to see which of your content is the most popular i.e. being re-pinned the most. Therefore, your business can understand what appeals the most to the public. Try to understand the patterns in content style and timeframe for rising popularity, and try experimenting with them so that you can understand how your content resonates with Pinterest users, and your clientele.

Most Clicked Content

The Most Clicked tab lets you see which pins are driving the most traffic from your Pinterest page to your website. This is obviously a great way to understand which content has the most potential for generating revenue, and also if the Pin It button is performing effectively. Once you know which pins are the most popular, you can create similar ones for your boards.

Although the amount of web traffic is a good indicator of how popular your business and content are on Pinterest, it is not an absolute method of doing so. Furthermore, becoming effective at making the right content on Pinterest takes time and effort. It is a slow process, but if you continue to study your Analytics, and identify patterns, you can create content which will drive more traffic to your boards and website.

CHAPTER 10

5 Marketing Musts for Pinterest

We have looked at several strategies which can help you increase web traffic to your site, and thus help spread your brand name. However, here we present 5 of the most important tips which any business should apply when using Pinterest to market their products and services.

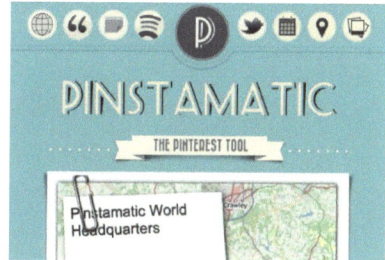

1. **Add a Pin It Button:** The whole point of a business being present on Pinterest is that they can spread their brand name and market their products among the countless Pinterest users out there. Repinning is the absolute measure of the popularity of your content, and the best way to make it easy for others to repin your content is to add a Pin It button to it. When they click on it, it will immediately pin the item to their Pinterest board.

2. **Use Pinstamatic:** Pinstamatic is a website which allows you to pin items to your Pinterest boards in an extremely quick and simple manner. Furthermore, it allows you to pin just about anything which you like

on the internet such as simple text, web-links, photos, videos, music, locations or even a Twitter account. This is an excellent way to add quality content in an aesthetically pleasing manner to your Pinterest board.

3. **Add Links to your Descriptions:** This is an absolute essential for anything that you pin. It makes it easier for the content to turn up on internet searches, and it also makes it easier for Pinterest users to find it. If you use a web-link in the description field for your content, and Pinterest recognizes it, then it will function as a back-link to your website as well.

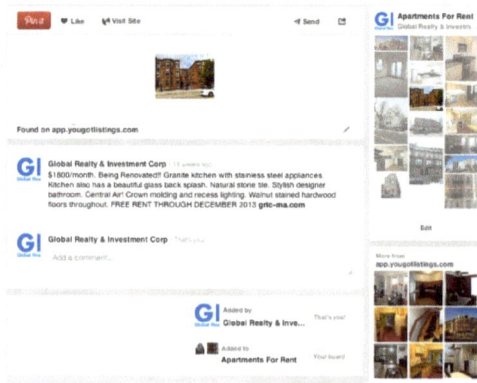

4. **Quality Text:** A typical Pinterest user will scan through countless pins and items before actually finding something that he likes. So try not to pin bulky, long-winded pieces of text. The best thing to do is to use text which has bullet points. These provide information in a much more clear and

concise manner, which appears visually pleasing to the viewer. Furthermore, research has shown that bullet point text is re-pinned more than regular text on Pinterest.

5. **Build your Community:** The concept of Pinterest, as with any other social networking site, revolves around this idea. The larger your online community is, the more people will see your pins when you upload them on Pinterest. A good way to do this is to repin from other peoples boards, join different communities, and thus add others to your own. Comment on pins which you really like, and others will comment on yours. Eventually, you and your business name will start to spread.

Follow these strategies and with time, you will begin to see your popularity on Pinterest rising. Keep an eye on your Analytics to see which of your content draws the most web traffic to your website, so that you can optimize it.

Show-off your Product

As an emerging business, you want your new products to gain the most popularity on Pinterest. You want them to get re-pinned by countless followers, and you want more web-traffic to be drawn towards your website. Here, we describe some ways in which you can really make your products stand out on Pinterest.

1. **Secret Boards:** The use of secret boards is an excellent way to create anticipation and eagerness among your clients and followers. Essentially, secret boards allow you to populate them with photos, items and other pins, before you make them public. Use secret boards to announce your new product, and use some clever photography to show its appearance from a certain aspect, without completely giving away the details. Then, when the time is right, allow the public to see the product. If you are lucky, this will draw immense web-traffic to your website.

Shhh!

2. **Good photos:** Having good quality photos on Pinterest is second only to having excellent content. Do not compromise on the photography or film-making equipment when you are marketing your products. You want to make a good impression on your audience, and a sure-fire way of doing this it to upload professional looking photos of the product. You could hire a photographer to do this for you.

Japanese Style

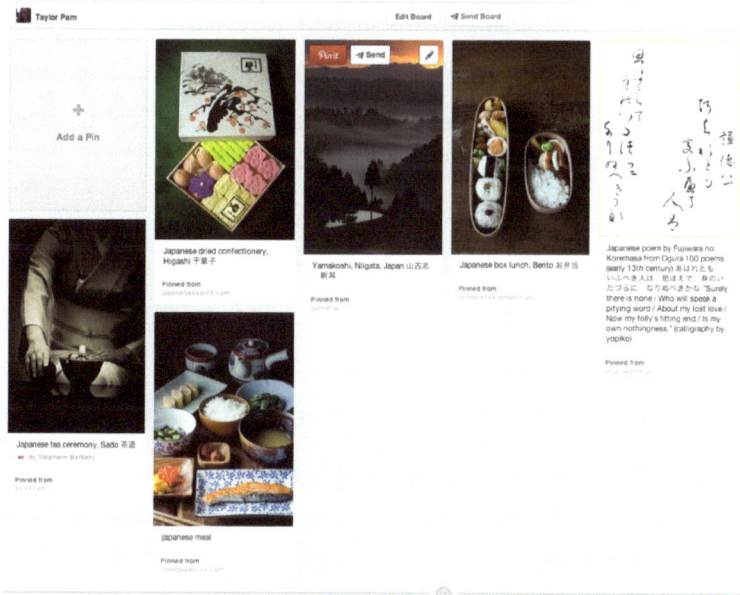

3. **Key words and descriptions:** Without appropriate descriptions, you will probably lose half of your potential followers without before they even click on your pinned and re-pinned items. Your descriptions should contain keywords, and they should describe in an interesting and informative manner, your new product. Try not to go into too much detail, particularly since you want to describe the salient features and benefits in your actual items and videos.

4. **Popular culture:** Associate your product with whatever trends are prevalent in the market. Make it the talk of the day by using iconic images and

symbols to your advantage. Show the public how your product keeps in with the popular cultural styles and fashions. If you can, try to set the new trend instead of following it. Your product will become truly legendary this way!

5. **Demonstration:** Give a demonstration of your product being used. Upload a video of customers using it on the streets and in their homes. Again, you can use pop culture to your advantage. Show the best features of the product which set it apart from its competition, but at the same time allow it to blend in seamlessly with the modern way of living.

By monitoring your Analytics, you can understand how much popularity a particular product has gained. You can even create a separate board for your most popular products. Add important details to their descriptions, and update them on a regular basis.

CHAPTER 11

Offer Deals

In this final chapter, we will take a look at some ideas for offers, discounts, deals and special packages, which you can offer to your clients through Pinterest, and how they can help improve your sales.

Promote Holiday Products and Packages

People go shopping whenever the holiday season is around the corner. Take this opportunity to increase your sales through Pinterest by promoting your holiday products. Create new Pinterest boards themed according to Christmas, Halloween, Thanksgiving, New Year or whichever holiday is coming up.

Show your audience how your products can add to the celebrations and festivities because of their features or themes. When pinning items from your website onto your Pinterest holiday boards, make sure the items lead to a page on your website where people can purchase the relevant item. If you slashed the prices of your products, make sure your descriptions mention this. Also, arrange your holiday product boards so that they are at the top of your Pinterest page.

Contests/Discounts

Run Offers and Discounts

People are drawn to discounts and special offers like moths to a flame! If you notice a product getting old, or receiving mild to low pins, then you might want to consider reducing its price. Make it accessible for more people, and someone is sure to purchase it. Pin photos of the item which you have put on a discounted price, and mention the new price in the description. Again, remember to link the item to the purchase page on your website.

https://www.facebook.com/pages/hop-at-Home/

Recently, GROUPGLOBAL.NET implemented a new way of promoting offers and discounts. When shoppers pin an item from the GROUPGLOBAL.NET website or the GROUPGLOBAL.NET Facebook page to their Pinterest boards with the tag #groupglobal, they unlock a special deal on that particular product. They have called it 'Pin It to Unlock', and prices for the special items were reduced by up to 70 percent. Try to come up with your own version of such a promotion, and it will surely be very popular on Pinterest.

Pin it to Win it!

Promote Affiliated Products

You can promote affiliate links and items from affiliate boards on your boards. Although it can be tricky sometimes, it is a good way to get some web traffic flowing through your Pinterest page. Make sure you verify any links before you pin them, and try to pin them from your review post.

On the whole, running offers and deals is a great way to boost your popularity. With rising popularity, you will draw more web-traffic, and thus more revenue through Pinterest.

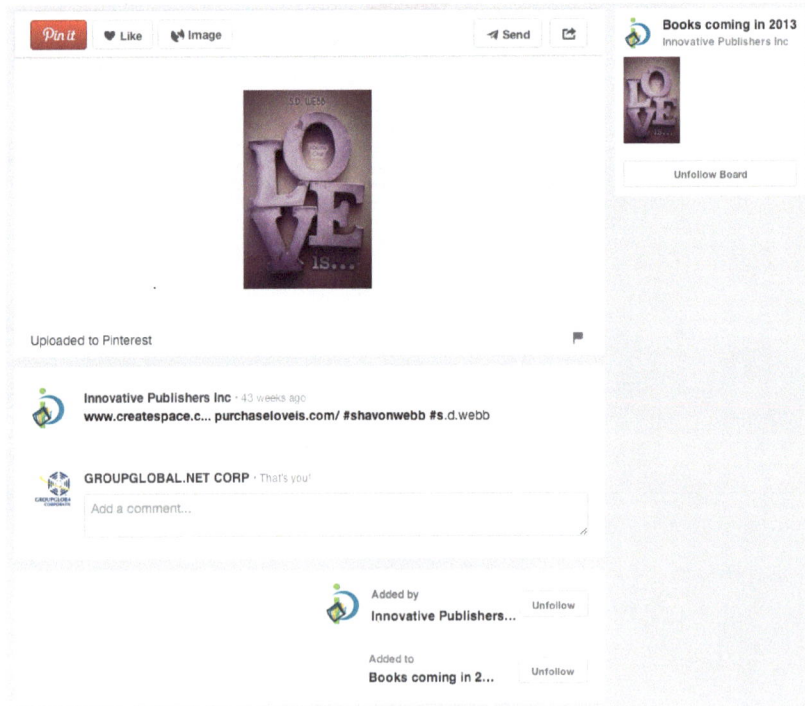

How to increase sales using Pinterest

Follow the companies and products showcased in this book:

GROUPGLOBAL.NET http://www.pinterest.com/groupglobalcorp/

- Office products, home and gift accessories

Global Realty & Investment Corp http://www.pinterest.com/gricma/

- Real estate sales and service

Intergalactic Travel Authority http://www.pinterest.com/itatravel/

- Travel agent and accomodations

Innovative Publishers Inc. http://www.pinterest.com/innovapub/

- Book and magazine publisher

Boston School of Real Estate Inc. http://www.pinterest.com/mabsre/

- Real estate school

Taylor Pam http://www.pinterest.com/mstaylorpam/

- Digital, acrylic and oil paintings

Love is... https://www.facebook.com/loveis.sdwebb

- Author (Love is...) and entrepreneur

Design Vendors

dsgn.io

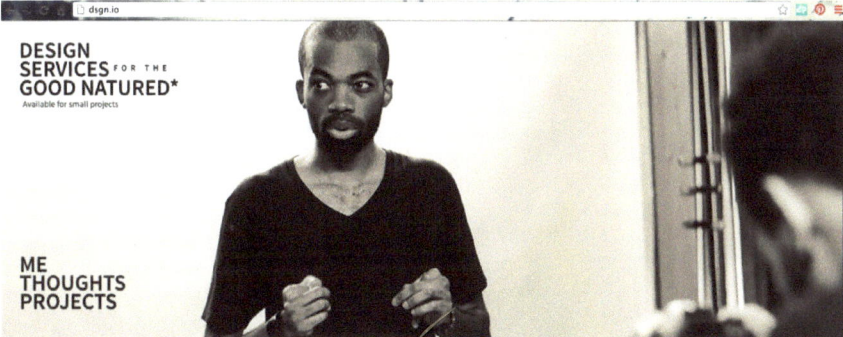

I am a proud lefty, Aries, and space bandit. The only pencil I trust is a Ticonderoga. I was born on Easter Sunday, 1988. I used to be an "Army-brat". My parents despised video games while I was growing up, so I am making up for it now (3DS, what's up?). I make music under various aliases, the most common being "the Wibby" (also FRSH×BTS and Spaceman Fresh).

I named my portfolio "Design Services for the Good Natured" because no one likes a jerk. Every day brings about new opportunities, inspiration, and kick-ass "whoah" moments. Spread the love and do your part by inspiring others as you've been inspired! (: That's what I try to do anyway.

https://twitter.com/NetOpWibby

http://dribbble.com/nokadota

Trademark Disclaimer

Innovative Publishers

Double Click Press